W9-BRR-116

SECRETS OF THE LOON

SECRETS
OF THE LOON

LAURA PURDIE SALAS
& CHUCK DAYTON

MINNESOTA
HISTORICAL
SOCIETY PRESS

Below white pines, at water's edge,
in guarded nest of mud and sedge,
squeezed inside an olive egg,
bill meets wing meets folded leg.

High overhead
    hangs a dawdling moon—
        then
            PECK! PECK!   WIGGLE!
A brand-new loon!

She's straggly and wet.
Soon the sun dries her coat.
She plops into water.

SPLASH!

Fear grips her throat.

Then the lake
sings its secret:

Moon Loon, you
can **FLOAT!**

Fish flip-flop and wriggle.
Loons shake first, then eat.
Moon's father gives demos:

SHAKE

SWALLOW

REPEAT

Moon gobbles up
minnows and crayfish —
delicious!

But an old turtle lurks,
its jaws
strong and vicious.

Moon Loon rides on Mother
side by side
with her brother.

Perched safely in feathers
    on Mama's broad back,
they rest out of reach
    of a snapper attack.

Summer wears sunshine or fog,
      soft and gray,
and skips by so quickly,
while Moon grows each day.

Eventually, Father's back
runs out of space,
so the chicks each tuck under
a one-wing embrace.

Lake wrinkles and twinkles
    below shimmering skies,
but danger flies over —
    with sharp, hungry eyes.

Mother's wild call, its rise and its fall,
warns Moon of the eagle.
    Can Moon Loon survive?

Her heavy bones whisper:

Moon Loon, you
can **DIVE!**

Moon dives underwater.
She glides, fast and sleek,
escapes the bald eagle's
talons and beak.

Cleaning
and preening,
Moon masters each skill.
She can catch her own dinner.
She fills her own bill.

Moon's learning loon music.
Mama's wail soars, haunting,
like the howl of the wolf,
full of searching . . .
of wanting . . .

Ooo- rooooooooooooooooooooo-
oooooo

One morning, two humans—
could they mean harm?—
venture closer.
And closer.
Father sounds the alarm!

His feet churn the water.
He rises, upright.
He calls, sharp and urgent,
   ready to fight.

After Father's aggressive
   and noisy display,
the humans quietly
   paddle away.

More lessons from Mother.

FLAP!

FLAP!

MOON LOON — TRY!

But a loon's built for water.
Leave the lake?

WHY?

These rocky shores, with trees tipped in gold.
These ripples and currents, fishy and cold.
This dazzling sky, a vivid blue dome.
This spruce-scented bay offers comfort.
It's home.

But early each morning,
Moon Loon flaps.

And fails.
Her narrow wings slap like weary ship sails.

Then one day,
she launches herself into sky.
Her wing feathers murmur:

Moon Loon, you
can **FLY!**

Wind whistles Moon's wings.
She is almost full-grown!

Soon her parents leave
Moon and her brother

all

alone.

The leaves flutter down.
Fall stamps them with frost.
Moon knows why she's going.
Moon knows she's not lost.

She'll fly through the breeze to warm, salty seas.
She'll stay

ONE

    TWO

        THREE winters
           where the ocean
             won't freeze.

Every secret Moon needs,
she carries inside,
and one late autumn morning . . .

MOON SPREADS
HER WINGS WIDE.

MORE LOON SECRETS

PATIENT PARENTS At age four or older, loons establish their summer nesting territory. Males and females share nest-building duties and sit patiently for nearly a month, regularly turning over one or two olive-colored eggs. Loon pairs return to their territory an average of five summers for hatching and raising chicks before moving on to a new territory. Nesting and hatching are almost the only times of their lives that loons spend on land.

LITTLE LOONS LEARNING Newly hatched chicks can swim, eat fish, and even dive. However, they tire quickly and face danger from snapping turtles and big fish, so they may ride on a parent's back for several weeks. Before climbing aboard, a chick might give its parent a little peck in the side; then the adult raises its wing. Riding on an adult's back keeps chicks warm and safe from dangers below. But sometimes eagles try to eat loon chicks. Loons are usually smarter and quicker. The adults sound a warning call, and the chicks dive quickly. When no predator is around, an adult might dive while a chick is sitting on its back, leaving the chick bobbing on the water's surface.

FABULOUS FISH CATCHERS With long, supple necks and sharp bills, adult loons are skilled fish hunters. If a captured fish is still wiggling, the loon shakes it hard, then gulps it down headfirst. Loon chicks love to eat, but they do not know how to catch fish at first. For hours at a time, the parent dives, catches a fish, then holds it in front of the hungry chick, which grabs it and swallows it in a flash. Repeat. Repeat. Repeat. When the parent stops, chicks sometimes bump against its side as if to say, "I want more fish." Soon, loon chicks learn to dive and catch their own food.

DETERMINED DIVERS Loons have heavy, solid bones and can squeeze the air out of their feathers. Both of those traits help them dive. They have special bodies for diving to help them drop fast and deep, staying underwater for up to four minutes. They can push the air out of their lungs and can even slow their heartbeat to use less oxygen. Below the surface of the water, loons hold their webbed feet sideways and use a froglike kick. As graceful as a ballet dancer, they shoot forward faster underwater than on the surface. By dragging one foot like a rudder, they can turn instantly.

FEATHER FUSSERS Loon chicks are born with fuzzy down, but by fifteen weeks they have a full set of gray flight feathers. Adult loons turn gray starting in the fall. In late winter, the adults molt, or lose their feathers, and then grow their striking summer plumage: black and white speckled back, white front, black neck stripe, and black head (which looks green in sunlight). To take care of their gorgeous feathers, loons preen, or clean and waterproof them. They pluck out any loose feathers and stretch up to spread their wings. Loons' bathing routine sometimes includes wild splashing to get rid of parasites. They also slide their sleek head to a gland on their back to get oil, which they smooth across their feathers.

CAPTIVATING CALLERS Loons use four basic calls. You can hear them at "The Voice of the Loon," listed on the next page.

WAIL A long, mournful call, sometimes three notes, which often means, "I'm here. Where are you?" A one- or two-note version is used to call a nearby mate or as a soft warning that people are too close. Chicks can produce only a soft, squeaky wail.

TREMOLO Like a slightly crazy laugh of short falling notes, the tremolo has several meanings. In flight, it announces a loon's location, such as an early-morning return from fishing on another lake. It can also be a warning cry at some sign of danger. And sometimes loon pairs sing a tremolo duet, their laughing calls echoing each other across the water.

YODEL The yodel is a territorial call made by a male loon. With his neck extended forward and his bill wide open, he calls loudly with a rising note first, then several short, harsh calls. The yodel announces, "This is my territory: stay away!"

HOOT These are soft and short calls. Chicks and adults hoot to each other a lot.

FANTASTIC FLYERS Those heavy bones that are great for diving make it hard to take off. Loons flap their wings and run a long way on top of the water to become airborne. Once they take flight, though, they fly very fast—up to seventy miles per hour.

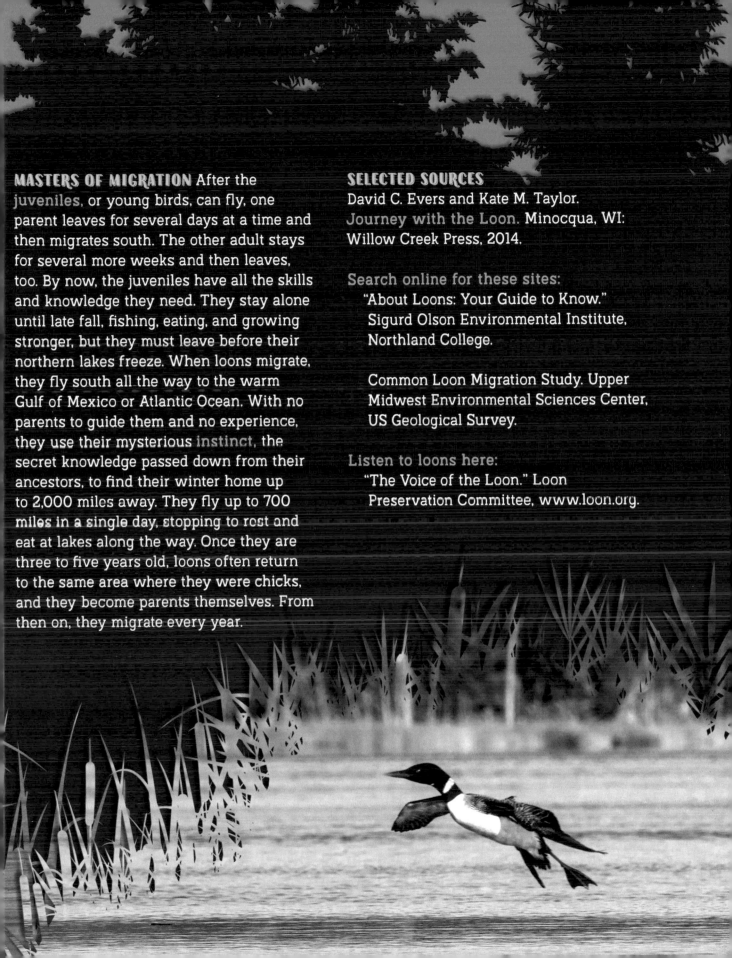

MASTERS OF MIGRATION After the juveniles, or young birds, can fly, one parent leaves for several days at a time and then migrates south. The other adult stays for several more weeks and then leaves, too. By now, the juveniles have all the skills and knowledge they need. They stay alone until late fall, fishing, eating, and growing stronger, but they must leave before their northern lakes freeze. When loons migrate, they fly south all the way to the warm Gulf of Mexico or Atlantic Ocean. With no parents to guide them and no experience, they use their mysterious instinct, the secret knowledge passed down from their ancestors, to find their winter home up to 2,000 miles away. They fly up to 700 miles in a single day, stopping to rest and eat at lakes along the way. Once they are three to five years old, loons often return to the same area where they were chicks, and they become parents themselves. From then on, they migrate every year.

SELECTED SOURCES
David C. Evers and Kate M. Taylor. *Journey with the Loon*. Minocqua, WI: Willow Creek Press, 2014.

Search online for these sites:
   "About Loons: Your Guide to Know." Sigurd Olson Environmental Institute, Northland College.

   Common Loon Migration Study. Upper Midwest Environmental Sciences Center, US Geological Survey.

Listen to loons here:
   "The Voice of the Loon." Loon Preservation Committee, www.loon.org.

For Lily and Logan, who were born to fly. —LPS

For Sara and the extended Dayton family who love Jasper Lake. May the next sixty-four years be as much fun, and may our special loons be present forever. —CD

With gratitude to Chuck Dayton and all those who work so hard to preserve our world's wild places. —LPS

Special thanks to Consie Powell for thoughtful critiques and encouragement, and to Johnna Hyde and Debra Frasier for their helpful suggestions. —CD

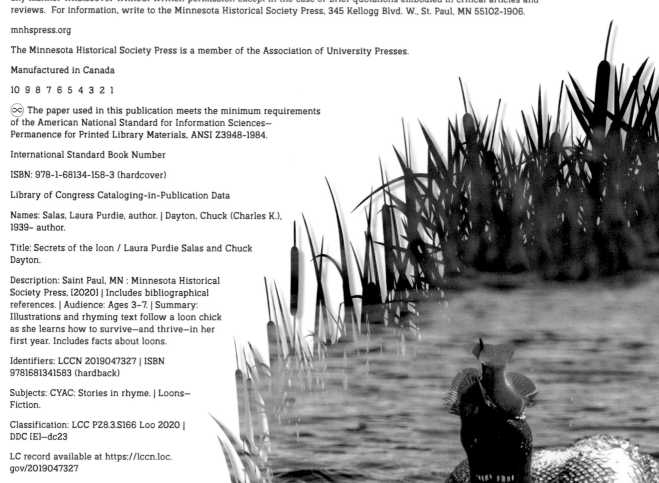

mnhspress.org

The Minnesota Historical Society Press is a member of the Association of University Presses.

Manufactured in Canada

10 9 8 7 6 5 4 3 2 1

♾ The paper used in this publication meets the minimum requirements of the American National Standard for Information Sciences—Permanence for Printed Library Materials, ANSI Z3948-1984.

International Standard Book Number

ISBN: 978-1-68134-158-3 (hardcover)

Library of Congress Cataloging-in-Publication Data

Names: Salas, Laura Purdie, author. | Dayton, Chuck (Charles K.), 1939– author.

Title: Secrets of the loon / Laura Purdie Salas and Chuck Dayton.

Description: Saint Paul, MN : Minnesota Historical Society Press, [2020] | Includes bibliographical references. | Audience: Ages 3–7. | Summary: Illustrations and rhyming text follow a loon chick as she learns how to survive—and thrive—in her first year. Includes facts about loons.

Identifiers: LCCN 2019047327 | ISBN 9781681341583 (hardback)

Subjects: CYAC: Stories in rhyme. | Loons—Fiction.

Classification: LCC PZ8.3.S166 Loo 2020 | DDC [E]—dc23

LC record available at https://lccn.loc.gov/2019047327